Tools

Search

Notes

Discuss
▶ MyReportLinks.com Books

Go!

PRESIDENTS

MARTIN VAN BUREN

A MyReportLinks.com Book

Susan Jankowski

MyReportLinks.com Books

an imprint of

 Enslow Publishers, Inc.

Box 398, 40 Industrial Road
Berkeley Heights, NJ 07922
USA

MyReportLinks.com Books, an imprint of Enslow Publishers, Inc.

Library of Congress Cataloging-in-Publication Data

Jankowski, Susan.
　Martin Van Buren / Susan Jankowski.
　　p. cm. — (Presidents)
　Includes bibliographical references and index.
　Summary: Examines the life of the lawyer politician who became the
eighth president of the United States and led the country through its
first serious depression. Includes Internet links to Web sites, source
documents, and photographs related to Martin Van Buren.
　ISBN 0-7660-5072-6
　1. Van Buren, Martin, 1782–1862—Juvenile literature. 2.
Presidents—United States—Biography—Juvenile literature. [1. Van Buren,
Martin, 1782–1862. 2. Presidents.] I. Title. II. Series.
E387.J36 2002
973.5'7'092—dc21
　[B]

　　　　　　　　　　　　　　　　　　　　　　2001004310

Printed in the United States of America

10 9 8 7 6 5 4 3 2 1

To Our Readers:

Through the purchase of this book, you and your library gain access to the Report Links that specifically back up this book.

The Publisher will provide access to the Report Links that back up this book and will keep these Report Links up to date on **www.myreportlinks.com** for three years from the book's first publication date.

We have done our best to make sure all Internet addresses in this book were active and appropriate when we went to press. However, the author and the Publisher have no control over, and assume no liability for, the material available on those Internet sites or on other Web sites they may link to.

The usage of the MyReportLinks.com Books Web site is subject to the terms and conditions stated on the Usage Policy Statement on **www.myreportlinks.com**.

In the future, a password may be required to access the Report Links that back up this book. The password is found on the bottom of page 4 of this book.

Any comments or suggestions can be sent by e-mail to comments@myreportlinks.com or to the address on the back cover.

Photo Credits: Photo Credits: © Corel Corporation, pp. 1 (background), 3; Courtesy of American Memory/Library of Congress, p. 28; Courtesy of Encarta, pp. 15, 41; Courtesy of MyReportLinks.com Books, p. 4; Courtesy of National Park Service, p. 25; Courtesy of PBS, p. 30; Courtesy of Seminole Tribe of Florida, p. 31; Courtesy of the Martin Van Buren Home Page, p. 42; Courtesy of the Museum of America and the Sea, pp. 32, 38, 39; Courtesy of White House History, pp. 19, 34; Department of the Interior, pp. 26, 40; *Dictionary of American Portraits*, Dover Publications, Inc., © 1967, p. 23; *Harper's Weekly*, p. 37; Library of Congress, p. 16; The Hermitage: Home of President Andrew Jackson, Nashville, Tennessee, p. 12.

Cover Photos: © Corel Corporation, White House Collection, Courtesy White House Historical Association

Contents

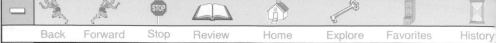

MyReportLinks.com Books
Great Books, Great Links, Great for Research!

MyReportLinks.com Books present the information you need to learn about your report subject. In addition, they show you where to go on the Internet for more information. The pre-evaluated Report Links that back up this book are kept up to date on **www.myreportlinks.com**. With the purchase of a MyReportLinks.com Books title, you and your library gain access to the Report Links that specifically back up that book. The Report Links save hours of research time and link to dozens—even hundreds—of Web sites, source documents, and photos related to your report topic.

Please see "To Our Readers" on the Copyright page for important information about this book, the MyReportLinks.com Books Web site, and the Report Links that back up this book.

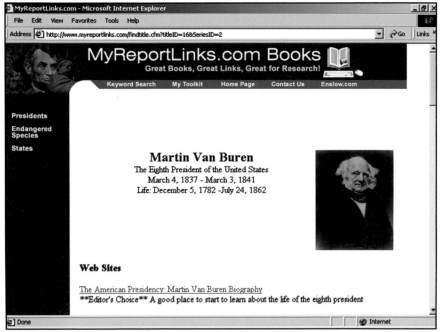

Access:

The Publisher will provide access to the Report Links that back up this book and will try to keep these Report Links up to date on our Web site for three years from the book's first publication date. Please enter **PVB1294** if asked for a password.

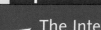
Report Links

➤ The Internet sites described below can be accessed at
http://www.myreportlinks.com

*EDITOR'S CHOICE

▶ The American Presidency: Martin Van Buren Biography
This site incorporates biographical information about Van Buren's early
life, Senate career, rise to the presidency, and his role as an elder
statesmen. It also includes links to his inaugural address, and a "quick
facts" section.

Link to this Internet site from http://www.myreportlinks.com

*EDITOR'S CHOICE

▶ The White House: Martin Van Buren
This official White House biography of Martin Van Buren examines
his life as the first president to be born under an American flag. His
vice presidency is examined as well.

Link to this Internet site from http://www.myreportlinks.com

*EDITOR'S CHOICE

▶ Martin Van Buren
A breakdown of facts about the eighth president, including the names
of his wife and children, the members of his cabinet, and the results of
the election of 1836.

Link to this Internet site from http://www.myreportlinks.com

*EDITOR'S CHOICE

▶ American Presidents Life Portraits
At this Web site you will find a letter written by Martin Van Buren to
his son in 1826 discussing his son's spending habits. You will also find
"Life Facts" and "Did You Know?" trivia about Van Buren.

Link to this Internet site from http://www.myreportlinks.com

*EDITOR'S CHOICE

▶ "I Do Solemnly Swear . . ."
This site contains memorabilia from Martin Van Buren's inauguration.
Here you will find photographs, arrangements for the inauguration
prepared by the Senate, and the text of Van Buren's inaugural speech.

Link to this Internet site from http://www.myreportlinks.com

*EDITOR'S CHOICE

▶ The American President: Martin Van Buren
This site is filled with information about Van Buren's politics, his wife
and family, life before and after the presidency, and his political defeat
and legacy.

Link to this Internet site from http://www.myreportlinks.com

Report Links

The Internet sites described below can be accessed at
http://www.myreportlinks.com

Angelica Singleton Van Buren
This Web site contains an exhibit dedicated to Angelica Singleton Van Buren. Here you will find a brief introduction to Singleton and a collection of books that belonged to her and her family.

Link to this Internet site from http://www.myreportlinks.com

The Aroostook War
In 1839, a boundary dispute between Maine and Canada erupted, resulting in an undeclared war. This site contains many links to informative sources about the Aroostook War.

Link to this Internet site from http://www.myreportlinks.com

Exploring *Amistad* at Mystic Seaport
This site explores the history of the *Amistad* revolt and the ensuing legal trial. Van Buren, at one time slave owner, had mixed feelings about slavery, which changed during his administration.

Link to this Internet site from http://www.myreportlinks.com

The First Roughshod President: Andrew Jackson
At the American Presidency Web site, you will learn about Martin Van Buren's early political career as secretary of state and vice President under President Andrew Jackson.

Link to this Internet site from http://www.myreportlinks.com

Hannah Hoes Van Buren
This site contains the biography of Hannah Hoes Van Buren. Although she died before Van Buren moved into the White House, she was said to have been a loving, sociable woman. Angelica Singleton filled the role of White House hostess.

Link to this Internet site from http://www.myreportlinks.com

Lindenwald: Martin Van Buren's Retirement Home
At this site you can view images and sketches of Martin Van Buren's retirement home in Kinderhook, New York.

Link to this Internet site from http://www.myreportlinks.com

Any comments? Contact us: **comments@myreportlinks.com**

Report Links

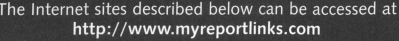

The Internet sites described below can be accessed at
http://www.myreportlinks.com

▶**Martin Van Buren**
Here you will find a brief biography of Martin Van Buren, which
focuses on his early political career and presidency. You will also find
links to his inaugural address and other presidential biographies.

Link to this Internet site from http://www.myreportlinks.com

▶**Martin Van Buren (Democrat)**
Van Buren's early life, career in the Senate, positions of secretary of
state and vice president, and his retirement years are discussed.

Link to this Internet site from http://www.myreportlinks.com

▶**Martin Van Buren: Inaugural Address**
When Van Buren was sworn in as president in 1837, his inaugural
speech indicated that he would continue in the direction that Andrew
Jackson had taken during his administration.

Link to this Internet site from http://www.myreportlinks.com

▶**Martin Van Buren (1782–1862)**
This site contains illustrations of Van Buren, and includes a small
biography which points out some criticisms regarding the eighth
president.

Link to this Internet site from http://www.myreportlinks.com

▶**Objects from the Presidency**
By navigating through this site you will find objects related to all the
United States presidents. You can also read a brief description of Martin
Van Buren, the era he lived in, and learn about the office of the
presidency.

Link to this Internet site from http://www.myreportlinks.com

▶**The Presidency**
At this Library of Congress Web site you will find original documents
relating to many United States presidents. At this site you can read a
letter written to Van Buren from Andrew Jackson, regarding the
nullification crisis.

Link to this Internet site from http://www.myreportlinks.com

 The Internet sites described below can be accessed at
http://www.myreportlinks.com

President Martin Van Buren
During the 1836 election, Van Buren won the majority of both the popular and electoral votes, easily winning the presidential race. This site has a chart that breaks down the votes for each candidate.

Link to this Internet site from http://www.myreportlinks.com

The Presidential Election of 1840
At this site you will learn about the Election of 1840. In this election, the Whigs triumphed with President William Henry Harrison defeating Martin Van Buren and others.

Link to this Internet site from http://www.myreportlinks.com

The Seminole Tribe of Florida
This site explores the history of the Seminole tribe of Florida, including the government's policies of displacement during the 1800s, and the American Indian resistance.

Link to this Internet site from http://www.myreportlinks.com

"The Star Spangled Banner" and the War of 1812
After the Revolutionary War, fighting with the British resumed in 1812 over territories and trade. Van Buren gained notoriety for prosecuting an American general who refused to fight in Detroit against an inferior British troop.

Link to this Internet site from http://www.myreportlinks.com

The Trail of Tears
As part of Jackson's Indian Removal Act, Cherokee Indians were forced to give up their land and migrate to another area, causing illness and devastation.

Link to this Internet site from http://www.myreportlinks.com

Van Buren, Martin
After a few months in office, Van Buren left his position as governor of New York to become the secretary of state in Andrew Jackson's administration. This site maps out his political road to the presidency, and contains six media items.

Link to this Internet site from http://www.myreportlinks.com

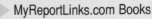
Report Links

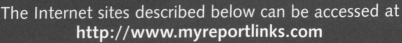
▶ **Van Buren, Martin**

The Encyclopedia.com Web site holds a brief biography of Martin Van Buren. Here you will learn about his early career, presidency, and later years.

Link to this Internet site from http://www.myreportlinks.com

▶ **Vice Presidents of the United States**

The "little magician," who appeared refined and well dressed, came from a working class family in upstate New York. He became a lawyer at the age of twenty-one, and then easily entered the world of politics.

Link to this Internet site from http://www.myreportlinks.com

▶ **Visiting Martin Van Buren's Grave**

Here you will find a description and image of Martin Van Buren's grave. You will also find links to other president's grave sites.

Link to this Internet site from http://www.myreportlinks.com

▶ **The White House Historical Association**

At the White House Historical Association, you can take a virtual tour of the White House and learn about the presidency. You will also find brief descriptions of all United States presidents.

Link to this Internet site from http://www.myreportlinks.com

▶ **Who was Martin Van Buren?**

Perhaps Van Buren's greatest achievement was to establish the Independent Treasury System, which protected federal funds.

Link to this Internet site from http://www.myreportlinks.com

▶ **1837–1841: The Eighth American President**

At this Web site, Martin Van Buren is characterized as "The Professional Politician." Here you can read a brief description about Van Buren and view a video clip.

Link to this Internet site from http://www.myreportlinks.com

Highlights

1782—Born in Kinderhook, New York, in the last year of the Revolutionary War.

1803—Becomes a lawyer. Admitted to New York Bar Association.

1807—*Feb. 27:* Marries Hannah Hoes, his distant cousin.

—*Nov. 27:* Son, Abraham Van Buren, is born.

1810—*Feb. 18:* Son, John Van Buren, is born.

1812—Elected state senator. War of 1812 against Great Britain.

—*Dec. 20:* Son, Martin Van Buren, Jr., is born.

1815—Appointed New York's Attorney General. War ends.

1817—*Jan. 16:* Son, Smith Thompson Van Buren, is born.

1819—Wife, Hannah, dies from tuberculosis.

1820—Elected to U.S. Senate.

1829—Elected Governor of New York. Soon resigns to become President Andrew Jackson's U.S. secretary of state.

1831—*June 25:* Appointed minister to Great Britain.

1832—Elected as Jackson's vice president.

1836—Elected president of the United States. Sworn in as president.

1837—Panic of 1837 banking crisis and economic depression.

1838—The *"Amistad Affair"* results in foreign policy crisis, and complicates the slave issue.

1840—Loses election to William Henry Harrison, a Whig.

1848—Runs for president on Free Soil Party ticket. Loses to Zachary Taylor.

1862—Dies at Lindenwald in Kinderhook from heart failure. Memorialized by President Abraham Lincoln and the U.S. Navy.

Chapter 1 ▶

Career Public Servant

Martin Van Buren was the first president to grow up knowing freedom. He was born in the last year of the Revolutionary War, just a few years after the United States declared its independence from Great Britain.

Van Buren's service to his country began in the court-room. He started out as a lawyer in his hometown of Kinderhook, New York. Van Buren's clever arguments, elegant dress, and red hair earned him the nickname, The Red Fox of Kinderhook. He later became a U.S. senator from New York, and finally, governor of that state. Van Buren then resigned as governor in 1829 to serve as U.S. secretary of state.

Throughout his career, Van Buren was a member of the Democratic Party. As secretary of state, he was a member of President Andrew Jackson's "Kitchen Cabinet." This was a group of politicians who helped Jackson plan ways to accomplish the goals of the Democratic Party. Van Buren's popularity among party members led him to become Jackson's vice president. This experience helped prepare Van Buren for the presidency.

During the presidential race, Jackson described Van Buren, a devout follower of the strict Dutch Reformed religion, as "a true man with no guile." In other words, Jackson told voters Van Buren was an honest person who would do his best to serve the country.

▶ Inauguration Day

On March 4, 1837, Van Buren rode to the White House in a coach made of timber from the American warship the USS *Constitution*. The ship withstood British fire during the Revolutionary War to help lead America to victory. The aging President Jackson rode in the coach with him. He and Van Buren's four sons looked on as their father was sworn in as the eighth president of the United States.

Hannah Hoes Van Buren, the president's wife, and mother of his sons, had died eighteen years earlier. Van Buren moved his sons and their families into the White House during his term.

In his inaugural address, Van Buren spoke to the American people with confidence. He boasted that the democratic system of government was strong and would serve as a model for all nations.

"Yet in all the attributes of a great, happy and flourishing people we stand without a parallel in the world," declared Van Buren. "America will present to every friend of mankind the cheering proof that a popular government, widely formed, is wanting in no element of endurance or strength."[1]

Van Buren vowed to carry on with Jackson's plans when he took office. He explained he wanted to provide America

◀ *As president, Van Buren hoped to follow the plans of the Jackson administration.*

with continuity. That promise was to fade during the next four years, as the policies Van Buren helped Jackson create erupted into crises.

By summer, America's banks would collapse and thousands would lose their land. Van Buren did not foresee that businesses would close and America would undergo an economic depression. The crisis became known as the Panic of 1837. To help solve the problem, Van Buren proposed the Independent Treasury Act. The act let the federal government control its money, rather than unstable private banks.

▶ Americans Divided on Slavery

When Van Buren took office, America was already divided on whether to grant civil rights to African slaves. Even though he had once owned a slave, Van Buren was from a Northern state. Thus, Southerners considered him to be a "Yankee." During his presidential campaign, Van Buren had promised Southern voters he would oppose the abolition of slavery. In his inaugural address, he reassured Southerners he would honor their wishes. He promised to block any attempts by Congress to free slaves.

As he delivered his speech, Van Buren had no way of knowing there would soon be a slave revolt that would make the situation worse. The revolt, known as the *Amistad* Affair, also caused tension between the United States and Spain.

The issue of slavery was the greatest challenge Van Buren faced as president. During his term in office, he changed his mind and came out against slavery. This decision cost him reelection to a second term.

Chapter 2 ▶

First Born in Freedom, 1782–1815

Martin Van Buren was the first president to be born a United States citizen. He was born on December 5, 1782, in Kinderhook, New York. Kinderhook was the setting for *The Legend of Sleepy Hollow*, the famous story by Washington Irving.

▶ Van Buren Follows the Founding Fathers

Van Buren's hero was Thomas Jefferson, one of the authors of the Declaration of Independence. On July 4, 1776, America's founding fathers declared "all men are created equal" in this document. Jefferson believed American citizens should be free to choose how they want to live. The idea that everyone has the right to be free became important to Van Buren over the course of his life. He made preserving American freedoms his life's work.

Martin was a small child when the founding fathers created the U.S. Constitution in 1787. The Constitution contains the laws that govern the United States. Washington became the first president when the United States of America officially became a nation in 1789. He appointed Thomas Jefferson secretary of state. Following in his hero's footsteps, Van Buren, too, would one day be secretary of state before he became president.

▶ Van Buren Learns from his Father

Martin Van Buren was born third of six children. His mother, Maria, also had two children from her first

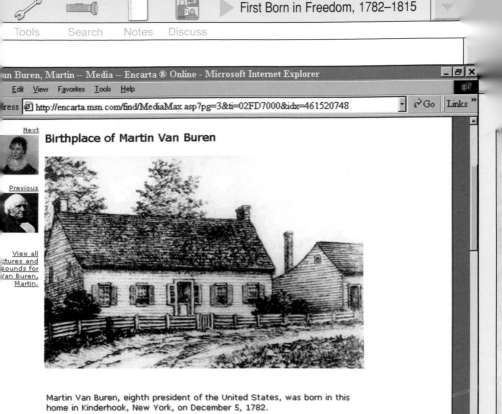

an Buren, Martin -- Media -- Encarta ® Online - Microsoft Internet Explorer

Edit View Favorites Tools Help

ress http://encarta.msn.com/find/MediaMax.asp?pg=3&ti=02FD7000&idx=461520748 Go Links

Next

Previous

View all
tures and
ounds for
an Buren,
Martin.

Birthplace of Martin Van Buren

Martin Van Buren, eighth president of the United States, was born in this home in Kinderhook, New York, on December 5, 1782.

Internet

▲ *Martin Van Buren's birthplace in Kinderhook, New York.*

marriage. Her first husband died many years before Martin was born. Abraham Van Buren, Martin's father, owned six slaves. Abraham was the town clerk. People came to him to take care of legal business. The Van Buren home was often crowded, with little room for privacy.[1]

Abraham Van Buren shared Jefferson's beliefs about government. Both men supported the rights of states. They wanted to limit the amount of control the United States' federal government had over its citizens. They believed that the U.S. Constitution should be strictly followed. As a boy, Martin listened to his father talk about these ideas.

Hard Work at an Early Age

Like most families in Kinderhook, the Van Burens were from Holland. They spoke Dutch, their native language, and attended the Dutch Reformed church. This religion stressed hard work and discipline for its members. From an early age, Martin helped support his family.[2] In addition to being the town clerk, Martin's father, Abraham Van Buren, owned a farm and a tavern. Martin often missed school to work for his father. When he was able to attend school, he and the other children read by candlelight. The small, drafty schoolhouse was not a comfortable place in which to study.

Beating the Odds

Martin had to stop going to school altogether in his mid-teens. He tried to make up for his lack of education in other ways. Van Buren was small, only 5-feet 6-inches tall, and struggled when he spoke in front of an audience. Since he had not studied at a college, he felt uncomfortable talking about certain subjects with men more educated than himself.[3] Eventually, Martin learned to overcome these hardships.

Kinderhook is near the city of Albany, so travelers stopped at the tavern. During the eighteenth century, taverns served meals and some rented rooms, like the motels of today. Van Buren heard guests talk about important news during dinner. One of them

Alexander Hamilton was one of many important guests that stayed at Van Buren's tavern.

was Alexander Hamilton, who helped write the U.S. Constitution. Guests and family members ate at the same table. Van Buren paid close attention to these men. He studied their ways.[4]

People rented rooms from Abraham for political meetings. The tavern also served as Kinderhook's polling place (the place where ballots are cast) during elections. The Van Buren home was at the center of the town's activity.

Some of the tavern's visitors were lawyers. Others were politicians or government officials. They talked about court cases and lawmaking.[5] Martin listened to their stories, and learned about justice in America.

As a teen, Martin worked as a lawyer's apprentice. His boss was a member of the Federalist Party. Political parties help people get elected to public office. Federalists wanted the American government to have more power to make laws. This view did not match Martin's ideas about government.

Yet Martin was on good terms with his boss. Back then, an apprentice would sweep the floor and tend the fire, as well as copy notes. Martin also used this job to educate himself on law and government.

To improve his appearance, Martin learned to dress fashionably. He wore clothes that made him appear taller. He attended parties to meet people. When he spoke, he chose his words carefully, and rarely lost his temper.

Good manners helped Martin make friends. He became popular, and his intelligence and charm impressed people.[6]

Like his parents, Martin worked hard, and planned for the future. He always researched a subject before he made a decision.

► The Little Magician

Sometimes people became angry with Van Buren because he would not give his opinion right away. But fiery action was not his style. Instead, Van Buren planned behind the scenes. When Van Buren achieved a goal, his success seemed to come from nowhere.[7] People joked that it seemed like magic. This earned Van Buren the nickname The Little Magician. Another nickname for Van Buren was Wizard. Still another was The Red Fox of Kinderhook because of his hair color and wit. Later, people would call Van Buren Old Kinderhook, or O.K.

Years of working for his father, then for the lawyer, taught Van Buren lessons about hard work and success. He earned the trust of people who shared the same ideas. With their help, Van Buren planned ways to solve America's problems. The Little Magician's "secret" was his determination to succeed.

► Van Buren and New York Grow Up

Van Buren became a lawyer in 1803 at the age of twenty-one. He joined the New York Bar, the state's official group of lawyers. Van Buren was known as an honest man, who chose cases based on right and wrong. The Little Magician was also quick to represent the common person.[8]

His law practice was growing along with towns in the Hudson River area. The invention of the steamboat drew people to the area. Many of them needed Van Buren's legal services. He was earning a reputation for being clever and capable.

After four years as a lawyer, Van Buren married Hannah Hoes, his distant cousin. He and Hannah grew up together. They shared the same lifestyle, but they had one

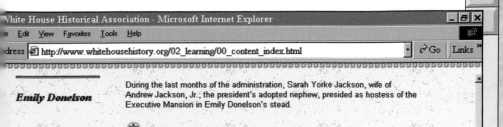

White House Historical Association - Microsoft Internet Explorer

File Edit View Favorites Tools Help

Address http://www.whitehousehistory.org/02_learning/00_content_index.html   Go   Links »

Emily Donelson

During the last months of the administration, Sarah Yorke Jackson, wife of Andrew Jackson, Jr., the president's adopted nephew, presided as hostess of the Executive Mansion in Emily Donelson's stead.

Cousins in a close-knit Dutch community, Hannah Hoes and Martin Van Buren grew up together in Kinderhook, New York. They were wed in 1807. Apparently their marriage was a happy one, though little is known of Hannah as a person.

Van Buren omitted even Hannah's name from his autobiography - a gentleman of that day would not shame a lady by public references. A niece remembered "her loving, gentle disposition" and "her modest, even timid manner." Church records preserve some details of her life; she seems to have considered church affiliation a matter of importance.

HANNAH VAN BUREN

She bore a son in Kinderhook, three others in Hudson, where Van Buren served as county surrogate. A fourth son died in infancy. In 1816 the family moved to the state capital in Albany. Contemporary letters indicate that Hannah was busy, sociable, and happy. She gave birth to a fifth boy in January 1817. But by the following winter her health was obviously failing, apparently from tuberculosis. Not yet 36, she died on February 5, 1819. The Albany Argus called her "an ornament of the Christian faith."

Martin Van Buren never remarried. He entered the White House in 1837 as a

error on page.   Internet

▲ *The president's wife, Hannah Hoes Van Buren, died of tuberculosis at the age of thirty-five. Van Buren never remarried.*

problem. In 1807, people in Kinderhook expected the bride and groom to invite the entire town to their wedding. This meant the couple had to feed hundreds of people.[9] The Van Burens could not afford to do this. As usual, Van Buren found a clever way to solve the problem. They held their wedding twelve miles out of town instead. Soon they moved to the larger town of Hudson. Later, the Van Burens had four sons: Abraham, John, Martin, and Smith Thompson.

Like other women of that time, Hannah's job was to care for the children and run the household. She did not become

involved in her husband's business matters. Her name does not appear in Van Buren's autobiography. In Van Buren's time, publishing a lady's name was considered disrespectful.[10]

▶ Champion of the Common Man

Even though America had won its independence, Great Britain was still a threat to liberty. In the War of 1812, the United States went to war with England again. British troops invaded Buffalo and Fort Niagara, New York. They set fire to many of America's government buildings in Washington, D.C., including the White House. Patriot Francis Scott Key wrote, "The Star Spangled Banner," America's national anthem, during this war. The war ended in 1815.

During the war, Van Buren served the people as a government official. At age twenty-nine, he was elected state senator. He was the youngest senator in New York. A few years later, Van Buren became New York's attorney general—the state's chief lawyer. He had truly become a powerful man.

Unlike others in government, Van Buren came from a common, working family. He helped common people by abolishing debtors' prisons. Before he helped change the law, people who could not pay their debts went to jail.

The Path to the White House, 1819–1836

Throughout his career, Van Buren kept close ties to his home state. He often worked on projects in New York and Washington, D.C., at the same time. People who shared Van Buren's views worked together to help him succeed.

▶ From New York to Washington, D.C.

Building the Erie Canal was one project that involved officials in both cities. Van Buren was New York's attorney general at this time. At first, Van Buren did not want to build the canal. He did not believe the federal government's money should pay for a project done in the state of New York.[1] Soon, Van Buren changed his mind. He decided the canal would be good for New York's businesses, which would help people in surrounding states as well.

The Erie Canal would run from the Hudson River to the Great Lakes. It would be ideal for transporting goods by ship. This would help farmers, tailors, ironworkers, and craftsmen. It would be a major construction project, requiring America's best engineers.

Once Van Buren agreed the canal was a good idea, he asked others to support it. He created a group to support the project. This group, known as the Albany Regency, quickly gained power. Its members convinced the local people that the canal would be good for everyone.

The Albany Regency was America's first political "machine." The group helped Van Buren achieve his goals for New York, even when he was away. People today

still use this term for groups that work behind the scenes for politicians.

By this time, Van Buren had moved his family to Albany. He was also spending more time traveling to Washington, D.C. Van Buren convinced five U.S. senators to vote in favor of the canal. Finally, the U.S. Senate voted to build the new canal. New York state would soon prosper. So would cities in the region.

New York's new governor, DeWitt Clinton, was angry with Van Buren because Van Buren did not support the canal from the beginning. This caused problems for Clinton. In the beginning, it had made it difficult for Clinton to get support for the canal.[2] When Clinton was elected to the governor's office, he fired Van Buren as attorney general.

When Governor Clinton fired Van Buren, many people became angry. These people, as well as Van Buren, became members of the "Bucktails" Party. Then, one of the Bucktails began working on the Erie Canal project. This helped Van Buren stay involved behind the scenes.

Soon Van Buren gained control over all the Erie Canal jobs. Anyone who wanted to work on building the canal had to join the Bucktails Party. This arrangement is called patronage.[3] The plan helped the Bucktails gain votes.

Today, there are laws against patronage in some places. Some people say it is wrong to trade jobs for votes. Others say it is simply a fact of politics. Some believe political parties protect citizens. They say that together, citizens can protect themselves against a central government that holds too much power. This was the view held by Van Buren. Not everyone shares this view.

The canal project would also make citizens in the state happy with Van Buren.[4] It would help him remain popular. This is important to people running for public office.

In the past, Van Buren helped other politicians run for public office. By doing this, he had learned that public opinion was very important to winning elections, and he knew what it would take to win them himself. In 1821, Van Buren was elected to the U.S. Senate.

Erie Canal construction was eventually completed on November 25, 1825. It made New York City the largest port in North America.

► Hard Times Hit Home

For Van Buren, his successes over that period of time were overshadowed by a series of personal tragedies.[5] Both of his parents, as well as his wife, Hannah, died during this period.

Hannah was ill before the birth of their son, Smith Thompson Van Buren. She suffered from tuberculosis. Hannah became even weaker after the baby was born. She passed away in February 1819. After Hannah's death, Van Buren turned to friends and family to help him raise four sons. Still, when Van Buren came home from work, he had many chores to do.[6] Although he survived his wife by forty-three years, Van Buren never remarried.

In a short time, Van Buren lost his parents, wife, and his hero. Former President Thomas Jefferson died on July 4, 1826. Former President John Adams passed away on the same day. This was also the fiftieth anniversary of the signing of the Declaration of

Hannah Hoes Van Buren. ►

Independence. Both men had signed the document. They had inspired Martin Van Buren, as well as his father.

Although Van Buren was busy at home, there was also political work to do. He rode his horse to late-night meetings in the cold, dark winter.[7] He and others in his political machine planned ways to win elections. They talked about solutions for America's problems. They read and wrote by candlelight, just as Van Buren had done when he was young. The cramped rooms where the meetings were held were not comfortable to work in.

The stuffy rooms Van Buren rented while traveling made him sick. Fresh air rarely entered these rooms.[8] Van Buren struggled with breathing problems throughout his life. However, he did not let sickness, the deaths of his loved ones, war, or other problems stop him. He was determined to preserve American liberty.

In the mid-1820s, Van Buren helped Andrew Jackson, a war hero, run for president. He convinced newspaper publishers to favor Jackson.[9] Like today, writers and illustrators helped shape people's opinions. For example, Van Buren and other presidents have been praised—and mocked—in cartoons. Meanwhile, Van Buren ran against DeWitt Clinton to become New York's governor. Both Van Buren and Jackson won their elections in 1828.

Clinton died shortly after the election. Even though the two had been enemies, Van Buren did not speak poorly of Clinton. Instead, he praised his foe's service to New York state.[10]

▶ A Step Up

When he was first elected, President Andrew Jackson was popular among Americans. On February 14, 1829, President Jackson wrote a letter to Governor Van Buren. In the letter, he asked Van Buren to become his secretary of state. This is an important office in American government. The secretary of state meets with world leaders to form agreements.

Van Buren's good manners, self control, and intelligence made him ideal for the job. So he accepted. After only forty-three days as governor, Van Buren resigned. His is the shortest term of any New York governor in history. Becoming secretary of state put Van Buren in the public eye of the entire country. Millions heard (or read) about Van Buren while he was meeting with foreign leaders.

This position also gave Van Buren the ability to influence government decisions. For example, Jackson asked

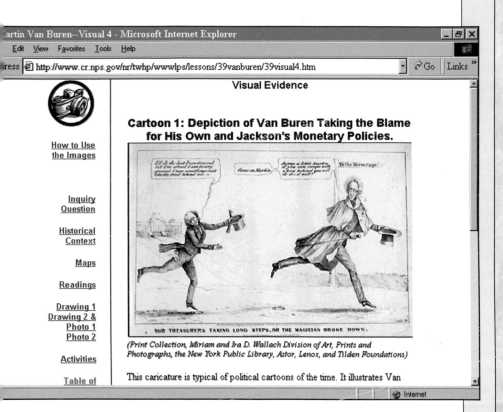

artin Van Buren--Visual 4 - Microsoft Internet Explorer

Edit   View   Favorites   Tools   Help

ress   http://www.cr.nps.gov/nr/twhp/wwwlps/lessons/39vanburen/39visual4.htm   Go   Links

Visual Evidence

How to Use the Images

Inquiry Question

Historical Context

Maps

Readings

Drawing 1
Drawing 2 &
Photo 1
Photo 2

Activities

Table of

Cartoon 1: Depiction of Van Buren Taking the Blame for His Own and Jackson's Monetary Policies.

SUB TREASURERS TAKING LONG STEPS, OR THE MAGICIAN BROKE DOWN.

(Print Collection, Miriam and Ira D. Wallach Division of Art, Prints and Photographs, the New York Public Library, Astor, Lenox, and Tilden Foundations)

This caricature is typical of political cartoons of the time. It illustrates Van

Internet

This political cartoon illustrates how President Van Buren took the blame for former President Jackson's financial misjudgments.

Van Buren's advice in selecting members of his Cabinet. This is a U.S. president's official group of advisors. Each member oversees different parts of America's government.

Jackson sought Van Buren's opinions often.[11] The two rode horses together. In many ways, though, they appeared to be opposites. Jackson was casual in dress and speech, while Van Buren dressed elegantly and spoke with caution. During his two terms as president, Jackson counted on Van Buren to handle important matters.

While in England on official business, Van Buren met Washington Irving, the writer who used Kinderhook as the setting for his book. He was also there on United States' business. The two became friends.[12]

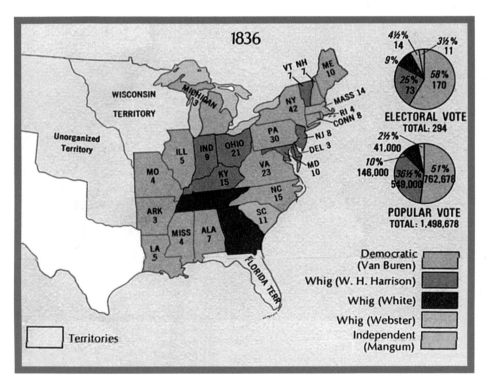

▲ This map shows the results of the presidential election of 1836.

Eye on the Oval Office

President Andrew Jackson won reelection in 1832. John Calhoun, the former vice president, resigned on bad terms. Calhoun had been Van Buren's rival.[13] Van Buren became Jackson's vice president.

Jackson, known to many as Old Hickory, was ill much of his second term. Van Buren worked in Jackson's absence. He often met with Democratic Party members. In 1836, Van Buren received the party's nomination for president. He worked hard to become America's top leader. He kept his sights on the Oval Office.

Van Buren promised to continue with Jackson's plans for the country. He even planned to keep the same people in the Cabinet. This is unusual. New presidents usually choose their own people for their cabinets.

Another promise Van Buren made in 1836 was to restore people's trust in the government.[14] People welcomed this message. In the 1836 presidential election, Van Buren beat out a trio of Whig candidates: William Henry Harrison, Daniel Webster, and Hugh Lawson White. The voters put their faith in Van Buren to solve some of the country's problems. Two of the biggest problems were different views on slavery and the shape of the American economy.

The Presidency, 1837

Van Buren officially became the eighth president of the United States of America on March 4, 1837. His vice president was Richard Mentor Johnson.

Van Buren rode to the celebration in a coach made of timber from the warship, the USS *Constitution*. This ship withstood British fire during the Revolutionary War.

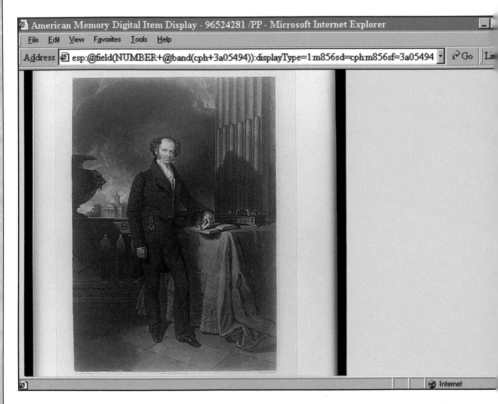

American Memory Digital Item Display - 96524281 /PP - Microsoft Internet Explorer

File   Edit   View   Favorites   Tools   Help

Address   esp:@field(NUMBER+@band(cph+3a05494)):displayType=1.m856sd=cph.m856sf=3a05494   Go   Li

▲ Martin Van Buren on the day of his inauguration. He was known for his impeccable dress and good manners.

Though ill, Jackson rode in the coach with President Van Buren. On this day the men were elegantly dressed. President Van Buren insisted Jackson remain at the White House until he was in better health.[1] This was unusual. Usually, the former president moves out when a new president is sworn in.

Sunshine Before a Storm

Although Van Buren had succeeded in becoming president, his hard work had just begun.

As the new leader, Van Buren faced challenges from the start. During Jackson's term, some of America's problems had grown worse. A weakened economy was causing people to lose their farms, businesses, and homes. A drought had ruined crops, and there were food shortages. This drove up prices, and the average person did not have enough money to buy food. As Van Buren took office, citizens rioted in New York. They demanded flour to make bread.

Some blamed Jackson for the banking problems, which had also weakened the economy.[2] When he was president, Jackson had stopped banks from giving credit. He did this to make sure the nation did not go into debt. This, however, made it more difficult for banks to do business. People could not get loans to buy lands in the West.

In addition, small wars were breaking out in parts of the country. United States' soldiers were fighting to help Texas win independence from Mexico.

In Florida, the U.S. Army was fighting the Seminole Indians in the Second Seminole War. In 1830, Congress had passed the Indian Removal Act. It forced American Indian tribes to move west of the Mississippi River. The tribes did not want to move away from their homelands, and the Seminole fought to stay.

Africans in America/Part 4/The Trail of Tears Close-up - Microsoft Internet Explorer

File　Edit　View　Favorites　Tools　Help

Address 🔗 http://www.pbs.org/wgbh/aia/part4/4h1567b.html ▾ 𝒞Go ‖Li

Done　　Internet

▲ *In 1830, Congress passed the Indian Removal Act. As a result, the Cherokee nation was forced to leave its land east of the Mississippi River. Unlike the Cherokee, the Seminole Indians refused to leave their land in Florida.*

A number of slaves who had escaped their owners fought alongside the Seminole. Some became members of the tribe. American troops were losing, because the Seminole knew how to survive in Florida's swamps. Desperate, United States troops tricked Seminole Chief Osceola. They set up a meeting to negotiate a truce. When Osceola came to the meeting, however, they captured him. In the end, not all of the Seminole moved. Some remain in Florida even today.

Despite these concerns, the mood on Van Buren's inauguration day was festive.[3] The weather was beautiful.

It must have seemed as though all was well in the United States of America. In the bright sunshine, there were no clues of a coming storm. However, in reality, America was headed for trouble.

Thousands watched Van Buren walk up the steps of the Capitol building to raise his right hand. Like every president, Van Buren vowed to uphold the U.S. Constitution.

People flocked to the nation's capital for the celebration. It included American Indians, who performed dances in traditional costume.[4] Many people came to listen to Van Buren's inaugural address. Like other presidents, Van

minole Tribe of Florida: Culture: Chickee - Microsoft Internet Explorer

Edit   View   Favorites   Tools   Help

ress   http://www.seminoletribe.com/culture/chickee.shtml   Go   Links

CALENDAR   GUESTBOOK   EMPLOYMENT   SITE INDEX
SEND EMAIL   SEARCH

Tourism   History   Culture   Archives   Home   Government   Services   Tribune   Market Place

Culture
who we are

Chickee

"Chickee" is the word Seminoles use for "house." The first Seminoles to live in North Florida are known to have constructed log cabin-type homes, some two stories tall, with sleeping quarters upstairs. The chickee style of architecture - palmetto thatch over a cypress log frame - was born during the early 1800s when Seminole Indians, pursued by U.S. troops, needed fast, disposable shelter while

MORE CULTURE
- Basketry
- Chickee
- Clans
- Seminoles and Christianity
- Dolls
- Green Corn Dance
- Seminole Food

Internet

▲ The Seminole Indians began constructing "chickees," a disposable shelter, in the early 1800s, when they had to run from persistent U.S. troops who wanted to remove them from their land.

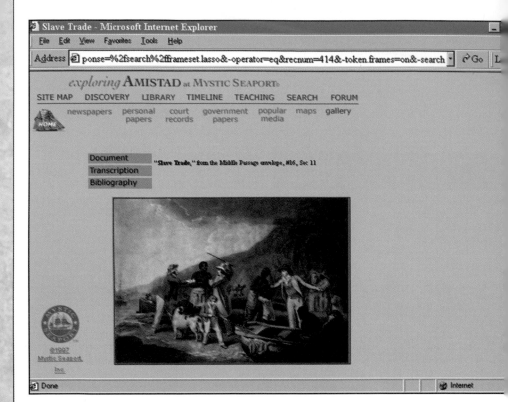

▲ This painting is an artist's depiction of the slave trade. Slavery was an issue that was dividing the United States.

Buren used his first speech to outline his plans for the next four years.

Basically, Van Buren planned to carry out Jackson's plans for the country. He had helped create these plans as Jackson's vice president.

▶ Inaugural Address

In his speech, Van Buren focused on slavery. Already, slave ownership was an issue that was dividing Americans. Van Buren promised to protect the right to own slaves in states that allowed it. Like Jefferson, Van Buren believed America's government should not interfere with states' rights. This pleased Southerners, many of whom were Democrats.[5]

Van Buren said he would work to restore citizens' trust in their government. In his address, he stated that America had the best government in the world. He spoke with confidence about the future. "Yet in all the attributes of a great, happy, and flourishing people we stand without parallel in the world," declared Van Buren. "America will present to every friend of mankind the cheering proof that a popular government, widely formed, is wanting in no element of endurance or strength."[6]

Keeping Peace in the New United States

President Van Buren moved into the Oval Office to begin many hours of hard work. America's problems loomed like a storm.

Van Buren's stand on slavery did not please abolitionists.[7] They did not think any state should allow slavery. They wanted to end it nationwide. As president, it was up to Van Buren to keep Americans from going to war over this issue.

Even though Van Buren had once owned a slave, he later changed his mind about the issue. Van Buren had owned a slave named Tom. When Tom ran away, Van Buren did not search for him. Ten years later, a man in Massachusetts found Tom. He bought him from Van Buren for fifty dollars.[8]

Van Buren did not call for an end to slavery while he was president. He did not want to prompt more arguing. Once again, people became angry with him for not taking a strong stand right away. He could not please anybody. People in the North, nicknamed Yankees, wanted him to stop slavery. Southerners wanted Van Buren to protect states' rights.

In the end, Van Buren decided slavery was wrong.[9] He worked hard to keep slavery from spreading to new territories and states.

There were also problems north of the United States border, in Canada. People in the southern part of Canada wanted to govern themselves. Many United States citizens joined Canadian troops to fight the British.

The Whig Party criticized Van Buren's plan to continue with Jackson's policies. They wanted to take away his power. Van Buren turned to his grown sons for help. They served as his advisors.[10] He sought their advice, along with

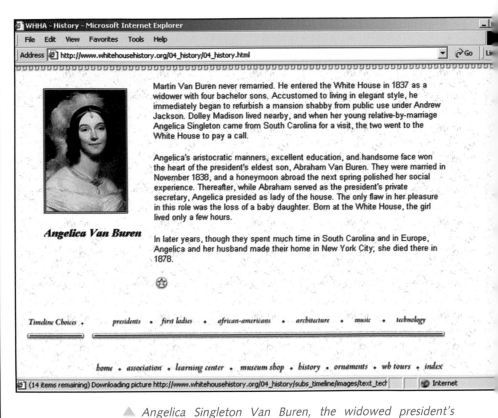

▲ Angelica Singleton Van Buren, the widowed president's daughter-in-law, served as his hostess.

that of Vice President Richard M. Johnson and Secretary of State John Forsyth.

Life in the White House

Two of Van Buren's sons moved into the White House with him. Soon Abraham married Angelica Singleton, daughter of a South Carolina plantation owner. Because Van Buren was a widower, there was no "first lady" in the White House. So Angelica became its hostess. She delighted guests by giving dinners, luncheons, and teas. Angelica performed this role until she gave birth to President Van Buren's first grandchild. Unfortunately, the infant died at the White House.

In addition to stylish clothes and fine food, Van Buren enjoyed dancing. The waltz was popular at that time. He attended dances with Jefferson's granddaughter, Ellen Randolph.[11] Van Buren liked talking about politics with family and friends. For Van Buren, dinners were social events, which could last for several hours.[12]

Van Buren also enjoyed horseback riding. He rode on and off the White House grounds. He often chose to ride a horse around Washington, D.C., instead of taking a horse-drawn coach.[13]

Chapter 5 ▶

Hard Times, 1837–1841

Several factors contributed to America's first depression. Crop failures, taxes on imported goods, and poorly run banks led to the crisis. Soon after Van Buren took office, foreign businesses pulled their money out of American banks. They were not confident about the strength of America's economy.[1] Also, the U.S. government had not printed enough money in previous years. There was not enough paper money circulating. This contributed to the crisis.

▶ The Panic of 1837

By summer, many American banks closed down. People called this crisis the Panic of 1837. Businesses and factories also closed their doors. Americans were soon homeless, hungry, and sick.

True to his style, Van Buren did not take action without doing his homework. He called a special session of Congress. The Senate and House of Representatives began working to end the depression. Van Buren presented a plan that would slowly solve the problem. America would establish its own Treasury, independent of banks. Van Buren believed America's money would be safer in the Treasury than in banks.[2]

Not everyone agreed with this plan, however. Whig Party members wanted to start a new national bank, instead of the Treasury.

Meanwhile, Americans were suffering. Many were without food or shelter. They complained that Van Buren

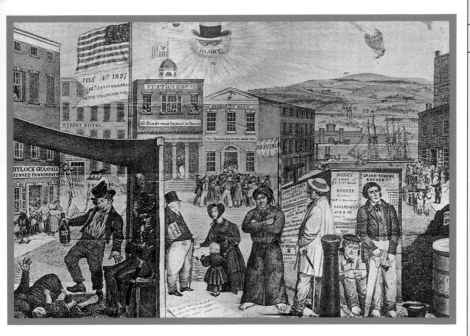

▲ This political cartoon illustrates that the Panic of 1837 caused many banks to close, affecting everyone from the prosperous merchant to the humblest laborer.

was not acting quickly enough. They accused him of forgetting about common people.[3]

The *Amistad* Affair

In 1839, two slave dealers paid Cuban officials to pretend fifty-two Africans were Cuban slaves. Offering money for a criminal favor is called a bribe. It is against the law in most countries. The dealers held the kidnapped Africans on a ship called the *Amistad*. During the ship's voyage to the United States, the Africans killed the ship's captain. They took over the ship and ordered the crew to bring them back to Africa. Instead, the crew steered to Long Island Sound, off the coast of New York.

An American survey crew captured the ship. They believed they were salvaging cargo.[4] The crew brought the

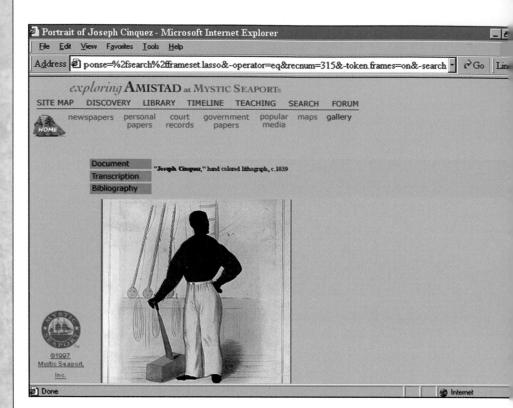

Document
Transcription
Bibliography

"Joseph Cinquez," hand colored lithograph, c.1839

©1997
Mystic Seaport,
Inc.

▲ Cinque led his fellow slaves in a revolt aboard the Amistad and killed Captain Ramon Ferrers.

Africans to New London, Connecticut, where they were held in jail. Runaway slaves were typically treated in this manner. Meanwhile, the slave dealers went to Spain to ask for help in getting the Africans back. Again they claimed the slaves were Spanish-speaking Cubans.

"The *Amistad* Affair," as it was called, created a problem for the United States with Spain. It also became a long court case. Spain asked America to return the slaves to Cuba, but an American judge took the bribery into consideration. He said the Africans were not really Cuban slaves. The case went all the way to the U.S. Supreme

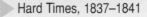
Tools   Search   Notes   Discuss   Go!

Court. The court ruled that the Africans should be freed. Thirty-nine of the slaves had survived the ordeal. Abolitionists raised the money to return these people to their homes in Africa.

▶ "The Log Cabin and Hard Cider Campaign"

At the end of his term, Van Buren received the Democratic Party's nomination for reelection in 1840. The Whigs nominated William Henry Harrison, a soldier.

The Whigs used Van Buren's fancy tastes against him. They knew he liked to drink expensive French wine. They said it was wrong to have fancy food and wine from

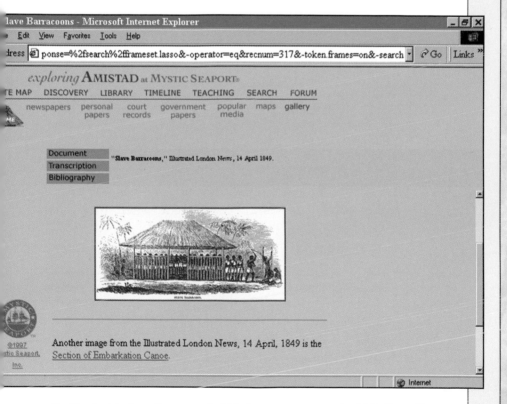

▲ The Amistad *captives were held in barracoons, or makeshift jails, until their trial.*

39

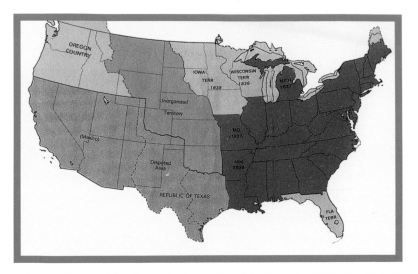

▲ By the time Van Buren had completed his term in 1841, the United States was undergoing major expansion.

Europe while Americans were starving. They said Van Buren should be drinking American-made apple cider instead. They pointed out that buying cider would help support common people.[5] They claimed he had been powerful for too long. They wanted to make it look like he was no longer fit to serve the country. One campaign slogan mocked Van Buren as "a used-up man" and an aristocrat.[6]

The Whigs' plan to make Van Buren look greedy worked. Newspapers printed negative cartoons about him. The Whigs' plan became known as "The Log Cabin and Hard Cider Campaign." It worked so well for the Whigs that even people in New York voted for Harrison. Van Buren lost the election.

Always a gentleman, Van Buren left the White House early, to give Harrison more time to move in.[7]

One month later, Harrison died. Vice President John Tyler became America's tenth president.

Chapter 6

A Change of Heart and Mind, 1844–1865

Van Buren did not win the Democratic Party's nomination for the next race in 1844. He lost because he did not want Texas to join the United States. He feared Texas would become a slave state. Van Buren also thought the annexation of Texas would further divide America, because now there

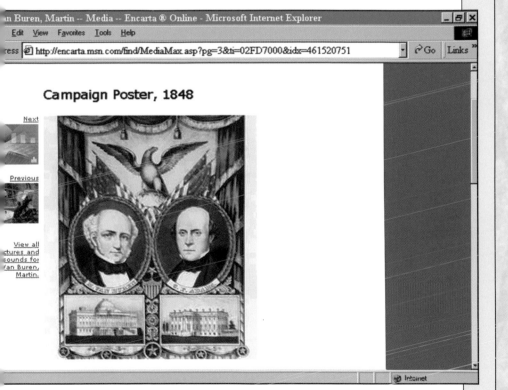

n Buren, Martin -- Media -- Encarta ® Online - Microsoft Internet Explorer

Edit   View   Favorites   Tools   Help

ress http://encarta.msn.com/find/MediaMax.asp?pg=3&ti=02FD7000&idx=461520751   Go   Links

Campaign Poster, 1848

Next

Previous

View all
ctures and
sounds for
/an Buren,
Martin.

▲ In 1848, the Free Soil Party nominated Van Buren for president. Although he did not win, he did capture enough votes from the Democratic Party to secure the presidency for Whig candidate Zachary Taylor.

would be more slave states than free states.[1] This view caused him to lose the nomination to James K. Polk, who became the eleventh president.

In 1848, Van Buren was nominated for president again. This time, he ran as the candidate for the Free Soil Party. Members of this party believed that new states and territories should not allow slavery. Although he did not win, Van Buren received more votes than expected.[2] Zachary Taylor eventually became the nation's twelfth president.

Lindenwald

Martin Van Buren 's Retirement Home

This is a picture of Lindenwald as it is today.

▲ *Martin Van Buren died at his farm, named Lindenwald, on July 24, 1862. The farm in Kinderhook, New York, is now a national historic site.*

▶ O. K.'s Last Days

During the first part of his retirement, Old Kinderhook, or O. K., relaxed at home in Kinderhook. He had named his 226-acre farm and estate Lindenwald. Later, Van Buren took vacations in Europe. He traveled to countries such as England, Italy, and France.

While in Europe, Van Buren heard about a possible civil war in America. States were threatening to separate from the U.S.A. So Van Buren returned to support Abraham Lincoln for president. Lincoln was a member of the Republican Party. Like the elderly Van Buren, Lincoln knew the importance of states' rights. But he, too, was against slavery.

In 1860, South Carolina separated, or seceded, from the United States. The Civil War began the following year. Union and Confederate soldiers were fighting on American soil. Hundreds died on the battlefield, under a sky darkened by gun smoke.

Van Buren died of heart failure at 2:00 A.M. on July 24, 1862, at Lindenwald. He had been sick with asthma for some time. Today, Lindenwald is one of America's national historic sites. President Abraham Lincoln wrote a passage praising Van Buren for his funeral.[3] He also ordered the U.S. Navy to honor Van Buren with an official salute.

Had Van Buren lived a few more years, he would likely have read Lincoln's Emancipation Proclamation. This document declared freedom for all slaves. He would have read the Thirteenth Amendment to the U.S. Constitution. It says, "Neither slavery or involuntary servitude . . . shall exist within the United States." This amendment was ratified by Congress on December 6, 1865.

Chapter Notes

Chapter 1. Career Public Servant

1. "Martin Van Buren Inaugural Address," *Grolier Presents: The American Presidency, 2000*, <http://www.gi.grolier.com/presidents/ea/inaugs/1837vanb.html> (May 25, 2001).

Chapter 2. First Born in Freedom, 1782–1815

1. John Niven, *Martin Van Buren: The Romantic Age of American Politics* (New York: Oxford University Press, 1983), pp. 6–8.

2. Ibid.

3. Ibid.

4. "President Martin Van Buren: Eighth President of the United States," *Thinkquest*, n.d., <http://library.thinkquest.org/12587/contents/personalities/mvburen/mvb.html> (February 20, 2001).

5. Ibid.

6. Major L. Wilson, The Presidency of Martin Van Buren (Lawrence: University Press of Kansas, 1984), p. 24.

7. James A. Beatson, "Martin Van Buren Biography," *Grolier Presents: The American Presidency, 2000*, <http://gi.grolier.com/presidents/ea/bios/08pvanb.html> (February 20, 2001).

8. Ibid.

9. Niven, p. 23.

10. "Hannah Hoes Van Buren 1783–1819," *The First Ladies*, n.d., <http://www.whitehouse.gov/history/firstladies/hvb8.html> (February 20, 2001).

Chapter 3. The Path to the White House, 1819–1836

1. Major L. Wilson, *The Presidency of Martin Van Buren* (Lawrence: University Press of Kansas, 1984), p. 26.

2. Ibid.

3. "Martin Van Buren: Eighth President 1837–1841," *The Presidents*, n.d., <http://www.whitehouse.gov/history/presidents/mb8.html> (May 25, 2001).

4. Wilson, p. 26.

5. John Niven, *Martin Van Buren: The Romantic Age of American Politics* (New York: Oxford University Press, 1983), p. 72.

6. Ibid.

7. Ibid., pp. 144, 192.

8. Ibid., p. 330.

9. Wilson, p. 132.

10. Ibid.

11. James A Beatson, "Martin Van Buren Biography," *Grolier Presents: The American Presidency, 2000,* <http://gi.grolier.com/presidents/ea/bios/08pvanb.html> (February 20, 2001).

12. Wilson, pp. 24, 115.

13. "Martin Van Buren: Eighth President 1837–1841."

14. Wilson, p. 301.

Chapter 4. The Presidency, 1837

1. Margaret L. Coit, et. al., *LIFE History of the U.S., Vol. 4: 1829–1849,* "The Sweep Westward" (New York: Time, Inc. Book Division, 1963), p. 32.

2. "The Princeton Economic Institute's History Dept," *PEI History Dept,* <http://www.nscds.pvt.k.12.il.us> (October 13–15, 2000).

3. John Niven, *Martin Van Buren: The Romantic Age of American Politics* (New York: Oxford University Press, 1983), p. 409.

4. Ibid.

5. Aileen S. Kraditor, *Means & Ends in American Abolitionism: Garrison & His Critics on Strategy & Tactics, 1834–1850* (Blue Ridge Summit, Pa.: Ivan R. Dee Publishers, 1989), p. 214.

6. "Martin Van Buren Inaugural Address," *Grolier Presents: The American Presidency,* 2000, <http://gi.grolier.com/presidents/ea/inaugs/1837vanb.html> (May 25, 2001).

7. Kraditor, pp. 162, 179.

8. Niven, p. 385.

9. Kraditor, p. 214.

10. James A. Beatson, "Martin Van Buren Biography," *Grolier Presents: The American Presidency, 2000,* <http://gi.grolier.com/presidents/ea/bios/08pvanb.html> (February 20, 2001).

11. Major L. Wilson, *The Presidency of Martin Van Buren* (Lawrence: University Press of Kansas, 1984), p. 23.

12. Ibid., p. 25.

13. Niven, p. 419.

Chapter 5. Hard Times, 1837–1841

1. "Key Events in President Martin Van Buren's Administration," *American Presidents: Life Portraits, 2000,* <http://www.americanpresidents.org/presidents/keyevents.asp?PresidentNumber=8> (May 25, 2001).

2. James A. Beatson, "Martin Van Buren Biography," *Grolier Presents: The American Presidency, 2000,* <http://gi.grolier.com/presidents/ea/bios/08pvanb.html> (February 20, 2001).

3. Ibid.

4. "The Amistad Case," *National Archives and Records Administration,* January 12, 1998, <http://www.nara.gov/education/teaching/amistad/home.html> (May 25, 2001).

5. Major L. Wilson, *The Presidency of Martin Van Buren* (Lawrence: University Press of Kansas, 1984), pp. 191–192.

6. Ibid.

7. John Niven, *Martin Van Buren: The Romantic Age of American Politics* (New York: Oxford University Press, 1983), p. 478.

Chapter 6. A Change of Heart and Mind, 1844–1865

1. "Key Events in President Martin Van Buren's Administration," *American Presidents: Life Portraits, 2000,* <http://www.americanpresidents.org/presidents/keyevents.asp?PresidentNumber=8> (May 25, 2001).

2. James A. Beatson, "Martin Van Buren Biography," *Grolier Presents: The American Presidency, 2000,* <http://gi.grolier.com/presidents/ea/bios/08pvanb.html> (February 20, 2001).

3. John Niven, *Martin Van Buren: The Romantic Age of American Politics* (New York: Oxford University Press, 1983) pp. 611–612.

Further Reading

Cole, Donald B. *Martin Van Buren and the American Political System.* Princeton, N.J.: Princeton University Press, 1984.

Ellis, Rafaela and Richard G. Young, ed. *Martin Van Buren: Eighth President of the United States.* Ada, Okla.: Garrett Educational Corporation, 1989.

Fitzgerald, Carol B., ed. *Martin Van Buren.* Westport, Conn.: Mecklermedia Corporation, 1987.

Hargrove, Jim. *Martin Van Buren.* Danbury, Conn.: Children's Press, 1987.

Jackson, Michael Weber. *Van Buren, Harrison, Tyler & Polk.* Vero Beach, Fla.: Rourke Corporation, 1996.

Mushkat, Jerome and Joseph G. Rayback. *Martin Van Buren: Law, Politics, & the Shaping of Republican Ideology.* Dekalb, Ill.: Northern Illinois University Press, 1997.

Myers, Walter Dean. *Amistad: A Long Road to Freedom.* New York: N A L, Division of Penguin Putnam, Inc., 1998.

Niven, John. *Martin Van Buren: The Romantic Age of American Politics.* New York: Oxford University Press, 1983.

Welsbecher, Anne. *Martin Van Buren.* Minneapolis, Minn.: ABDO Publishing Company, 2001.

Wilson, Major L. *The Presidency of Martin Van Buren.* Lawrence: University Press of Kansas, 1984.

Zeinert, Karen. *The Amistad Slave Revolt & American Abolition.* North Haven, Conn.: Shoe String Press, Inc., 1997.

Index